Cross-Training

Cross-Training

*An exploration in thirteen fits
of the "hidden years"
of Yeshua Natzrati
undertaken by*

Dennis Marden Clark

WAKING LION PRESS

Cover: *Calming the Storm.* by Simon de Vlieger, oil on canvas, 1637

ISBN 978-1-4341-0544-8

© 2021, 2023, 2024 Dennis Marden Clark

Printed in the United States of America

Published by Waking Lion Press, an imprint of the Editorium

Waking Lion Press™ and Editorium™ are trademarks of:

The Editorium, LLC
West Jordan, UT 84081-6132
www.editorium.com

For the forms of name in the following narrative
I follow the Hebrew and Aramaic as established
by David Stern[1] in his *Complete Jewish Bible*
in the "Pronouncing Explanatory Glossary."

---

1. As regards pronunciation, Stern says "The guttural stop *alef* is represented by an apostrophe (') before a vowel, except at the beginning of a word (example: Natan'el is pronounced Naetant'**el** and not Naatat**nel**). The stronger guttural stop *'ayin* (closer to the hard "g" sound) is represented by a reverse apostrophe (') before or after a vowel."

Although I use the Aramaic form "Yeshu" for the name we now speak as "Jesus" in our American English, on occasion I use the Hebrew "Yeshua," as his compatriots may have done.

Contents

viii

They'll no' get him a' in a book I think
Though they write it cunningly;
No mouse of the scrolls was the Goodly Fere
But aye loved the open sea.
["Ballad of the Goodly Fere," by Ezra Pound]

Fit 1

Yeshu was young when he went yondering,
leaving Miryam memories of youth,
leaving Yosef yearning with knowledge,
leaving his brothers bereft and lonesome,
leaving his sisters silent and mourning,
leaving his neighbours knowing, relieved.
Jesting, he joked that as a journeyman,
a carpenter coming to practice his craft,
as unsure as a shaver shoving his knife,
where he'd end up, or when return.
He was walking away to win the world,
worth of that world the weight of yonder,
the lure of wandering widely abroad.

Yeshu took lingering leave of Yosef,
the father who fostered and fastened his craft,
taught chisel and mallet, chamfer and drawknife,
use of plumb-line and eye to examine
the straight of the lintel and narrow of latch—
mate plank to plank, bond board to beam

join and true jamb and hinge,
so door will swing wide to welcome,
close to shelter kids and kin,
latched against the legionary,
open to neighbours, to all Natzeret.

Yeshu bade Miryam his mother goodbye,
knowing hers the womb that bare him,
knowing hers the paps that fed him,
that gave him suck—and succor when hurt,
and hers the voice that verified
the love of heaven he heard all about,
in songs of birds, in bursts of wind
among the corn and shaken barley,
in skitter of mice amidst the thatch,
scent on the breeze of mustard bush,
smoothness of shaven and sanded plank.

Of Ya'akov, the brother next younger than him
he asked a boon "Bless our father
who came out of Egypt, carried us home—
with all of your aid in every task,
spend your strength to succor him."

To sisters and brothers younger he said
"I will remember until I return
your faces and voices, visage and stance.
Bless your mother with moments of peace.
Fight if you must but not with Miryam."

His tools were stored and strapped in his box.
The food his mother had fixed was stowed

among the chisels, mallets and drawknives.
He strapped the box to his back and stood,
then stepped through the door and started to go.

His family swarmed and foamed about him,
answered his farewell admonitions
with advice, and with versions of visions he'd shared—
though never the one that ate at his nerves
on days he was quiet and quick at his labors,
when eager to fend off the fear that one fed,
the one that drew him to drift and seek.

Yeshu sought apprenticeship
to a master of vine, a merchant of oil
whose vineyard and grove were gravely in need
of care, the grafted shoots agog—
vines overgrown, grape gone to vine,
the olives alive, but little on the branch.
He found a poorly place in Ramatayim,
half-a-morning's walk from Yerushalayim,
finding lodging with a fellow Natzrati,
then offered to fix the gate in the fence
for Yosef the master, young though he was.

Willing to serve, to work as new fingers
for Yosef whose knowledge was locked in knuckles
swollen with age and stiffened by labor,
Yeshu presented himself to the master
as one who knew the shaping of wood,
one who could grasp the grain in its growth,
could pare from the living olive the punied

twig, the dying branch, the withered
limb, the shape of water shoots,
to shape the vine as vessel for wine,
to bleed the vine and bless the grape,
weep with the vine and waste no grape—
to shape the bunch through bitter loss.

"I am a worker in wood. Are you willing
to teach me the ways of trees and vines,
to know the heart and heft of wood,
the grain and growth, the give and grab,
how wind shapes wood, how water sculpts
branch and bud, bough and vine—
how soil will shape and sun reform
the limb, the bunch, the leaf, the fruit,
and when the knife is needed to shape,
the fingers to pinch and guide the growth
that brings the grape, the olive, to bear?"

"Will you bear the sun beating on you?
The wind from the west that wastes the vine?
the locusts who leave no leaf on the vine,
the armies that steal stem and oil?
If so, I'll sketch that skill for you."

The master then asked the most important
matter his mind was muttering over
this young one seeking, this Yeshua:
"Are you not he who was heard in the temple
at twelve instructing the Tz'dukim masters,
not two years past, distressing your parents?"

"I am. My aim in answering
the learned fathers of Yerushalayim
was to learn how little lore I'd absorbed,
how line upon line I'd learned the word,
but had I heard the heart of it beat?"

Master and student started their labors,
Yeshu content to serve a year,
Yosef at heart hoping for more.

Working under Yosef's words,
fingers flexing to form the grape,
blade swift and sharp to prune
the olive where growth allowed a graft,
Yeshu was never not conversing
with Yosef, as often he'd yakked with another
Yosef, but never mindless noise.
This one had heard the youth as he spoke,
knew the grasp of his growing thought,
understood the oddity
this boy had seemed to boys and men
in Natzeret—a knowledge that grew
with every night's meal and dreams.

Yeshu shared with Yosef the dream
that gnawed his nerves, the one he'd never
told to Miryam, or made his siblings
wince to hear, the one that woke him,
the one that drew him to drift and seek.

Together the boy and the grandfer reshaped
the runners, the knobs, the nubs of the vine,

moving through winter's withering cold,
shaving the shoots and shafts aimed at light;
shaping each cluster to cleave to the sun—
yet welcome the shade of leaves in summer
that drink in sunlight and swell the cluster
of grapes, that grab for growth from the ground.
Mere knobs in the air—the promise of increase
awaiting embrace of warming breezes
and water not wasted in winter's despite.

The olives alive in root, but not limb—
they cut the death from depths of the wood;
then from lively limbs of wild trees
pared out green shoots and grafted them in
to the dying tree to try their strength.

Yeshu asked Yosef "How shall we know
when we have grown and grafted in
enough to know the needful done?"
Yosef rejoiced to join to this youth
his knowledge of prophets known from his studies,
of Tzenos the husbandman, Tzion his subject,
the people of God grown as a vineyard.
"Have you Yeshu heard the words
of Tzenos the prophet, the parable he preached
likening Isra'el to an olive tree,
a tame and husbanded tree in a vineyard
pruned and dunged and digged about
which grew, waxed old, began to decay?
Tonight, when we rest we'll read from his words."

His labor was lighter with the lure of that promise
leading his thoughts, lighting his sight
as he struggled to shape and shift the tree
from the one at his face to the one in his head.

Shaping the tree, Yeshu searched
his memory, mindful that Tzenos
was not a name he recognized.
At meat that night, "Master" he said
"Tzenos is not a name I know
among Nevi'im from memory or study.
Did not Yirmeya chastise Yerushalayim
for welcoming profane priests and prophets
to counsel and serve sanctuary and king?"

"Tzenos the prophet, Tzenock the poet,
were sent by Yahweh to Yosef's seed
in Eretz Yisra'el, the land of Yosef—
the kingdom that was, Assyria's captive,
the wealthy exiled, carried far off.
Such was the fate of my family, who settled
in Cyprus, as traders before trickling back
to our homeland, to find Shomron infested
by settlers sent from Assyrian kings.
Long have my kin labored, as we
today have dug and dunged and grafted
to bring our land to life again,
to bring our lives to the land again.

"Let us search, Yeshu, the story
Tzenos the prophet tells of his Lord,

who grew a vineyard and groomed therein
an olive tree alike to mine.
When it grew old, began to decay,
he pruned it, dug about and dunged it,
until it began to tickle the breeze
with tender leaves somewhat a little."
He brought a scroll, began to recite
as if, in the Temple he read from the Torah,
singing the phrases surely, exactly:

Behold, the height, the heft, of the olive
began to decay, killed by its years.
The master saw, and said to his servant
"Pluck for me branches borne on an olive
wild, by the way, one in its vigor,
and we will pluck the withering branches,
fling them into the fire to burn—
while I will take of the tender and young
shoots of this tree some, to shape
the nether parts, the poorer soil,
to save the fruit, preserve this tree.

The servant gathered and grafted the branches
from wilder trees to the tamer olive.
The master took its tender shoots
from the favored olive afar in the vineyard,
planted them there to prosper and grow
in the nethermost parts, in the poorest soil,
and tended and nourished the newer trees.

"Now, Yeshua can you see

in this parable how the parallels
between our labors and the Lord's
mark the way that we must go,
define our duty to fill our time?"

"Yes, Master Yosef—But is that all?"
The boy was puzzled by such a preaching.
"The Lord of the vineyard transplanted one limb
to a good patch of ground, where it grew,
like the others, but only one part grew well.
The other part produced wild fruit.
The Lord told his servant to pluck the unsavory
branches and burn them. But the servant said
'Let us prune it and dig and dung it longer.
Perhaps we can help it and harvest good fruit.'
Master relented, let servant work.

"But Yeshu, now you should be able
to see the way Tzenos set forth
the Master's love for his many people,
how he has planted wherever he would
the branches that should bring him good fruit.
When next the servant and master inspected
the vineyard they found the fruit all corrupt:
the tame tree, the transplants,
had all produced dubious olives,
the taste on his tongue torture to the Master.
He was minded to burn this burden of care."

Yeshu was silent a short time
then spoke to Yosef: "Did not Yesha'yah

when he told of the vineyard show the Lord's temper,
who felled its hedge, made a wild field,
not to be pruned or raked, plucked or tended—
though the men of Isra'el were the Lord's vineyard?
And that was before Babylon fell."

"Yesha'yah saw the sins of his city.
Tzenos took the tree in the vineyard—"
"Master Yosef, that makes me wonder
why plant olives in part of the vineyard?
We have labored long on the vines,
but Tzenos ignores the grape and its wine
in this tale he tells of futility."

"Yeshu, my son, the olives serve
as windbreak, to temper the tempest from the east,
to shelter the vine from the sun at dawn.
Olives will grow where grapes will not;
on rocky soil they send forth shoots.
The Lord of the vineyard found that the olives
please him more greatly than grape or wine.
To me, the sweet wine swelling the grape
is better than the bitter olive in its brine,
and even fermented the grape pleases more.
The olive tree takes seven years
to bear its fruit, and further seven
before it reaches its full youth."

"Yosef, might I liken myself
to the olive tree? For I have lived
that long and now have left the vineyard,

"And does not Micah, a mouthpiece of God,
say: *And it shall happen in future days*
that the mount of the Lord's *house shall be firm-founded*
at the top of the mountains,
lifted over the hills.
And the people shall flow to it,
and many nations shall say:
Come, let us go up to the Mount of the Lord,
and to the house of Jacob's God,
that He may teach us of His ways
and that we may walk in His paths.
And He shall judge among many peoples,
arbiter to nations from afar.
And they shall grind their swords into plowshares
and their spears into pruning hooks.
Nation shall not raise sword against nation,
nor shall they learn war anymore.
And they shall dwell each man beneath his vine
and beneath his fig tree, with none to make him tremble,
for the mouth of the Lord *of Armies has spoken.*
For all the people shall walk
each in the name of his god.
But we shall walk
in the name of the Lord *our God*
forevermore.
"I chose to leave, to change my living,
search out and find the fig and the vine,
the promise of peace and prosperity
wherever the Lord my God shall lead me.

"And Yeshu, the Yesha'yah
you ask about, was sent to the south
when Eretz Yisra'el, the land of Yosef—
the kingdom that was, the captive of Assyria,
fell, to warn the fellows here,
but in his singing did not recite
the promise made from Micah's mouth.
So both can bless your brow with wisdom
and help you heal the hurt you fear,
to know the word that brings you weal,
that led your feet to live with us.

"You left your vineyard to toil with me—
left your family, and father and mother
to find new parents—to act apprentice
where you are needed now, with us,
For Marta and I—more fond have grown
of you, and more in need of youth—
You have become akin to us."

"Much have I learned, Master, from you.
I feel this kinship—it fills my heart.
How many times did the Lord relent
and try to keep the tree alive?
How many servants sent he to the vineyard?"

"The Lord accepted his servant's pleas
and planned once more to prune and to nourish,
to tend the good fruit and toss the bad—
but Tzenos says though the servant brought
other servants, they were scarce, were few.

They labored alongside the Lord mightily,
obeyed his orders in all their efforts
until again there began to be
natural fruit of the native tree—
which pleased the Lord yet left him leery,
fearing his olives would fail again
and leave him finally to fire the vineyard,
to burn the vineyard to very ash."

"How sad" said Yeshu; "and yet he saved
much of the fruit, preserved the faithful
root to the final fiery end.
So wide the world, so much of waste."
Yeshu wept for the wild fruit.

Yosef and Marta moved at the sight
embraced the boy, embarrassed the boy,
and yet he cleaved and clung to them—
and now Yeshu knew what next
lay before him: a journey to find
those other shoots of the mother tree,
wherever the Lord had left them to grow.
He knew what he did not know, but must learn
in furthering his apprenticeship:
to build and keep a one-man boat
workways with the wind and the waves.

Fit 2

Yeshu was young when he went yondering,
left Yosef and Marta marred with his going
though bearing their love as a burden of light,
and a letter to Marta's mother in Tzidon
where he was sure he'd find a shipwright
in need of a worker who'd know how wood
could best be worked with little waste,
one whose labor could pay for learning,
who'd willingly work while the sun shone,
with the strength of youth and the skill of craft,
whose hands knew the grain and heft of a beam.

Much it cost him moving away,
carrying love as load and leaven—
but he also bore his box of tools
and a solid beginning in grounds and soils,
his pay for the toil of trimming and pruning—
and a bronze knife bought in the market.
He guarded closely the gold in its closet,
hidden in the box he bore on his back,

mureera worth as much, or more,
and white-streaked líbanos, Lebanon stock,
wrapped well to keep the fragrances fresh.

His track to Tzidon with many travelers
nourished his plans with knowledge and hope,
talking with others who trekked that way,
while camping at dusk, at dawn when resuming,
sharing the food that Marta had fixed,
that Yosef had given from grapevine and olive,
that he had bought from burghers at market—
dates and figs and fruits without stones,
breads and water, wine and oil
he freely gave and got alike—
a welcome host, worthy companion.

This caravan of travelers
came first to Tzor, to Tzidon next—
in both these cities he sought and found
room at the inn where he could rest,
wash, and refresh his face and clothes.

Yeshu slept in the sand that night
and in the morning asked about
after a boatwright willing to take
an apprentice, proper proof of mastery.
The first he approached proved obstinate,
the second already arrayed in help,
and so throughout a weary day,
asking after the master,
to serve as carpenter, learning to shape

wood to float, to carve the waves—
till finally one, in friendly tones,
asked where he lodged, with whom he lived;
he answered "With Marta, mother of merchants,"
the only name he knew in Tzidon
mother of Marta in Ramatayim,
"Though I'm a craftsman, a carpenter—
I come to learn, to live by learning:
gleaming and gloaming I gather my tools
to work or to rest as my worth may determine."

"And what would you learn from your willing work?"
"To build a ship to sail to Tarshish.

"To build a boat that's big enough
to sail the open sea for trade
or seeking fish, and fleet enough
to fly before the flowing wind—
the storm astern, the stillness come—
bouyant like cork, bright as a bubble,
clear as the sun and silent as death
to bear but one alone on the waves."
"Give me a year and your full attention
and I will teach even a peasant
carpenter to craft such a vessel,
one that fisher or farmer could keep
workways with the wind and the waves."

Washed at an inn, with clothes shaken out,
bearing the letter from Marta and Yosef,
he went to the market to seek her mother,

find direction to her door,
seek a roof where he might rest.

Herself a merchant with sons and servants,
a widow, yet still with skill and wealth
working to fit her family for Rome
and Roman rule in Eretz Y'hudah,
and all around the world as known—
she welcomed him as worthy to dwell
with family and guests as friend and kin.

She asked her guests to give account
each of himself, his family, his town.

"I am Shaul shaped of Tarsus,
studied Torah as Parush at Temple,
studying Torah, Nevi'im, Kethuvim,
words and wisdom and witness of the LORD.
Of the party of Tzadok, people of the Temple.
A maker of tents, I make my own way
in the world of men; I work with my hands
and mind in designing and making from cloth
the shelters for souls who shoulder their burdens
and travel for trade or treat with their peers,
That is who I am. And who, boy are you?"

"Born in Beit-Lechem, exiled to Egypt—
my parents returned to the town of their marriage,
to Natzeret, where they were known—
where I learned the craft of carpentry
from Yosef, my father—and from my mother
Miryam the meditation

on hope and love that lifts and heals.
I worked with the olives at Arimathea,
to shape and to nurture, to share and to graft.
I know the bones of bole and bough.
I've come to learn the craft of boats,
building of ships shaped for the sea.
I'm bound for Tarshish; not to trade or flee,
as Yechezk'el or Yonah either.
I will need sails to move such a ship.
Can you make them as you make tents?
Can you share and shape the ship of my intent?"

"And you, young son can you spend anything
but breath on my cloth and my labor to catch
the breeze as it blows and billows my stitches?"

"And what is your fee for a full-fledged tent
to stand in the wind and withstand the whirlwind?
How much do you ask? For your efforts, and makings?
For cloth tightly woven in warp and in woof,
that can furl and unfurl, what your fee, what the cost?
What price do your ask for your efforts, your pains?
For such cloth, such a sail,
foe to wind, friend to sun,
twisted cotton, tight woven,
source of shade, shape of home,
reinforced to reef and furl?"

"I see you have words to match your will,
and you have enough knowledge about
my trade to pique my interest.

I also work in wool and leather
and I can craft such cloth to sail
as I have done a dozen times
in my days here—and all have held
for fishermen and freighted craft.
The fee for such a sail is steep
and must be held by whom I trust:
three golden Caesars, whole and solid."

Marta asked "My sons, am I
trusted enough by each of you
to hold the coins that cover this work?"
Both buyer and merchant agreed the bargain;
Yeshu promised payment in a week.

Akamas assigned Yeshu a task:
"Have you ever used
a shaving horse Yeshu, to smooth
a board or beam without waste?"
"My father," he said "had such a tool
and taught the use of it to me."
"I want you to make one fit to this work,
modeled on mine but built for your body,
with which you can shape planks for a ship
to fit to its ribs fixed with bronze nails,
or trunnels from olive or cedar trees."
From their barrow inside his box
Yeshu took the token coins
showed them to Shaul, gave them to Marta
when Shaul agreed they met his price,

but told to none the origin.

Yeshu began to build, measuring
himself against the horse of Akamas,
then watching the master work a plank
for a lapstrake hull light and buoyant,
and then selecting thick and sturdy
logs and posts for legs and saddle
and starting to shape them to a shave horse.

At meal that night he made his labors
known, and how his horse was shaping.
Shaul was laughing—and shared his pleasure:
"I come from Tarsus, center of trade,
Its university universally renowned.
Born a Roman, blessed with Paulus—
imperial name. But the pride of Tarsus
belongs to an earlier emperor.
Your work with that horse conjures his
in taming Bukephalas. That's how he came
to conquer the world, his work the battle."

"This is a tale I've not heard told,
two-named Paulus. Pray, tell on."

"Bukephalas was branded with the head of an ox.
No man could tame and mount this horse,
despite their spirit, for his was greater.
But Aleksandros was no man,
merely a boy of barely twelve—
quick to observe, slow to approach.
He spoke to the horse soothingly,

turned its head toward the sun
so it could no longer see its own shadow,
that black beast whose mimicry blasted
its peace, its pride, its privilege.
His fluttering cloak he cast aside,
mounted and rode that rogue, that horse."

Yeshu knew the nature of Rome
that it ruled through rumour and reigned by fear,
no one allowed to live in peace,
no one to work his will, her way,
but always fear the blade, the flay,
and wondered whether this Alexandros
had ruled the world in such a way.

Day after day as he tamed his horse
shaping it to Yeshu himself,
the scene of that story strutted again,
staging itself in the shelter of the tent
where he could shape and shave and smooth.

He planned to seek out cedars of Lebanon
when ready to create his craft, of his craft,
to sail the open sea for trade
or seeking fish, and fleet enough
to fly before the flowing wind—
the storm astern, the stillness come—
bouyant like cork, bright as a bubble,
clear as the sun and silent as death
to bear but one alone on the water,
a tiller of olive to turn the boat

workways with the wind and the waves.

He knew the blessing of blade, of edge
employed and put to proper use,
not drawn to show the shine of pride.
Learning to shave, to shape a shaft,
to plane a plank, prepare a board
to fit a hull to house a fisher,
he had the heart of wood to heed,
that told the scorp to scrape just so,
and showed him how to hold the blade
to fit that plank to rib and prow,
or steam and shape the shaven tree.

At meat one night Shaul asked Yeshu
if he could mend the loom and shuttle
so necessary, needful, now
but gnawed by thread finely twined,
by cotton, linen, leather, wool
and snagging now on woven cloth.
"Can you amend and meliorate?"

Yeshu answered Shaul "I will
seek out the wood and take the measure
and tell you then what cost you'd face."
When he'd finished his enquiries,
he told the toll: a basswood frame
and loom well smoothed for warp and weft,
an ironwood shuttle, shaped for speed,
smoothed against snags, a hefty heddle
and pedals to push it up and down

to keep the warp tight on the weft—
for this, two Caesars golden and whole.

The price agreed, Yeshu sought
the best of those woods, worked or rough,
and early went to work the parts,
to shape and fit to Shaul's frame
the better tool, new and sturdy.

When he had mastered the horse and knife
and built and bettered the loom for Paulus,
Yeshu used those early hours
before Akamas named the task
the day required—and with his assent—
to shape the spokes and shafts and rims
for wheels to rig and roll a wain
large enough for logs enough
to build a boat big enough
to sail to Tarshish swift on the sea,
and on to Ouiktis and wider seas.

For use of the wain for five years,
Yeshu rented a yoke of oxen
and training to drive the team with tact
and firmness, fitting the flick to the beast,
calling each ox to haul with the others.
"I see I can trust you with my team
since you would know from Adam's off ox."

He guided the wain to the wilds of Lebanon,
led by foresters who aided all fellers
where he hugged and heard the hearts of cedars,

the limbs of lime trees listening,
lingered long to learn of them.

Yeshu showed his chosen trees
up in the wild woods of the mountains
to foresters whose aid he trusted,
who sent Yeshu shinnying up
the trunk to log the limbs and lower them
that no wood be wasted,
the limbs for planks, the trunks for keel
and thwarts to bear mast, deck and tiller,
a mast to bear and master the sail
a spar to hold the sail to the wind
and ribs to shape with adze and steam.

His apprenticeship now at its end,
he and Akamas set forth to learn
to build this boat bouyant like cork,
bright as a bubble flowing on a brook,
clear as the sun and silent as death
to bear but one alone on the water,
one to tread the sea to Tarshish.

And as they labored from day to day
the young one learned what he'd already learned,
to split a plank from a slab of trunk
already split, one shaped by the tree,
or shape a kelson to strengthen the keel
that cuts the waves for a carvel hull
and a tiller of olive from a dying tree.

And when he made time to make other

tools for Shaul who was shaping his sail;
they paid for that labor—he got back the gold.

They shaped a luzzu, a ship for the sea,
and when it was launched, it floated upright.
They clambered aboard and Akamas taught
the lubber to tack and twist against
the wind, to sail straight by going
crooked, catch the wind in its clever
well-woven sail. Sometimes
Shaul came too with Akamas
to watch Yeshu learn a different
craft, to dodge the swinging yard,
and not be knocked head over heels
over the gunnel and into the sea.
Often they sailed out to sea
and back to shore until Yeshu
was competent and confident
to sail into the setting sun
workways with the wind and the waves.

Fit 3

Yeshu was young when he went yondering,
braving the world in a purpose-built boat,
bearing his tools and wealth in a box
safely stowed beside the back bow,
along with a letter from Marta of Tzidon
to her brother's son, a merchant in Ouiktis,
a buyer of bronze and dealer in blades.

When he went to Marta to settle accounts
she told him Shaul had paid for his month
of learning to sail—a parting gift,
in part the pride of a master weaver
seeing his sail set in the wind.
The separation of soul and soil
accomplished, he set out to sea.

Still sailing for Tarshish, then open sea
to visit the source of vital alloys
to satisfy curiosity
perhaps to learn metallurgy,
or maybe to find a new horizon.

From scraps of ironwood Yeshu shaped
spiral screws to secure in the beach
at the edge of the tide, as he worked on the loom,
not willing to waste wood or labor;
the screws he secured to thwarts in the ship
by sturdy lines to strain against
the ship at anchor, secured by a stone
on the seaward side of the sleeping boat,
the sail furled, its sailor asleep,
the screws defended about their base
by tribuli, obtained through trade,
a Roman trap deployed to ruin
the feet of camels, of elephants.

His life, his labor for two long years
had fit like a puzzle, two seasons of labor
dawn till dusk doing each task
fitting each plank plumb with another
on Akamas' contract or on his own,
work in winter to warm his muscles,
working in summer to sweat himself
until he could launch his luzzu himself,
when wind came walking upon the water.
One fellow worker gave him a fish net
when he departed, one he had given
his shave horse, who could work on it—
who showed him how to rig the net.

Wild waves washed wood,
net would fill with fish as he sailed,

tacking against a western wind,
or driven by drafts flowing abaft;
He'd trade the fish for bread and wine.

Some nights when he had no fish to trade
he'd sail on, aimed at a setting star
in the west, the one his mother Miryam
told him had hailed his birth, and brought
magi from Persia with the gold, the mureera,
the líbanos, his worldly wealth, with little
but hints in his heart of how he would spend it.

One day, off Kyrĕnē he hauled his catch
onshore to share and swap for food,
and met a man whose trade was metal—
Shim'on, a Roman Jew like Shaul,
who'd sailed one time to see the sources
and meet the makers of metal, his bronze—
but not to Ouiktis, where Yeshu was aimed,
but Kernow, where tin and copper together
have grown in God's grace and succor.
Yeshu shared the missive from Marta
to Dāwīd ben Yehuda, son of her brother.
"Seek him not in Ouiktis, my son,
for he now dwells in Aberfala."

"And where would I find this Aberfala?"
"It lies along the coast of Kernow
where Fala flows to fill the sea,
east from Belerion, the land's end.
These are the names you'll know it by.

At Karthāgō you must not stay
as you have done to trade with us,
but pass it by. There pirates dwell.
And pass Tarshish and its pillars of stone
and coast the north shore till it curves
north, and you navigate by the great bear,
passing Olisippo that ancient port
and one where you may safely rest."

"These names I now know, but how shall I know
this Kernow, and its Belerion?"

"On our voyage, my shipmaster
asked of the Franks after Olisippo,
who told him when to sail the sea
which stars to steer by on the open ocean.
If you have truly come from Tzidon
this far, then that will be within
the realm of the possible for one of your skill."

One final favor Yeshu frankly
asked: "How can I deploy
these tribuli to guard my sleep?"
and showed the sharp foot-shatterers.
Together Shim'on and Yeshu planted
the things in the sand below the tide,
and both slept the better that night for that.

So Yeshu sailed as Shim'on advised,
avoiding places where pirates might hide,
seeking more help when stopping to trade,
moving by day, mainly, and anchoring

to sleep, away from centers of trade.
One night, a scream of pain shook him
awake; he saw a youth bent double
on the sand, and sobbing shaking his foot.
He swam to shore and held the screamer,
and with his hands worked out the hook,
and healed the foot with prayer and faith,
and asked what she had aimed to do,
what deed she did in the dead of night?

"I saw your boat. Thought there might be
food aboard for my family and me.
Didn't think of booby traps."
Yeshu swam back, hauled up the stone,
then back again, and with her help
hauled the boat in and gave her all
the food on board, sent her away.

When she was gone he freed the boat
set sail again, steering for the star
that heralded his birth and rarely after
stayed anywhere near sandy beach
until he reached Olisippo,
and there he rested seven days,
observed Shabbat with merchants there.

He sailed again, coasting the shore,
until he found the Franks he'd heard
Shim'on expound, and explained
where he was bound. They bade him
"wait until in the clear of night

the wind comes walking upon the water,
then aim by the bear and sail full out
until you see Belerion
and then turn eastward, coast the shingle
of Kernow till Fala flows to the sea.

The merchants there will welcome you."
And so it proved, when he set out,
the separation of soul and soil
a trial until he saw the shore,
and sailed until Aberfala
hove into sight, keeping himself
workways with the wind and the waves.

Fit 4

Yeshu was young when he went yondering,
coasting Kernow, several stadia
off the shingle seeking Aberfala,
leery of submerged boulders shed
off cliff or brae, cleve or scarp,
the burden of Roman tribuli borne
like an anchor stone around his heart.

He sailed, his back to Belerion
thus for several days and nights,
sleeping at anchor with sail furled,
restlessly riding the rise and fall
of tides crashing on pebble and cobble
until he reached a calmer flow,
and Aberfala with other people.

The folk of the city welcomed this fellow
blown in off the ocean burdened and haggard,
and when he said in his halting Greek
that he was a Jew, had sailed from Tzidon,
they led him cross town to a synagogue

where he showed the letter from Marta, the mother
of Marta Ramatayim, they summoned for him
Dāwīd ben Yehuda, who was wary, until
he'd studied the missive this wanderer showed him,
had asked how things fared with Marta his aunt,
and heard how Shim'on, had shepherded him.

"You know who I am. But who, son, are you?"

"Born in Beit-Lechem, exiled to Egypt—
my parents returned to the town of their marriage,
to Natzeret, where they were known—
where I learned the craft of carpentry
from Yosef, my father—and from my mother,
Miryam, the meditation
on hope and love that lifts and heals.
I worked with olives at Arimathea,
with Marta, your cousin, and her husband Yosef,
to shape and to nurture, to share and to graft.
I know the bones of bole and bough.

"And then to Tzidon to learn of boats,
the building of ships shaped for the sea.
I built the one I came here on,
not to trade or flee, as Yonah fled.
I seek a tree that summoned me."

"Your life is like one long apprenticeship.
This tree you seek—is it for timber
it draws you here where Druids reign?"

"I built that ship from cedars of Lebanon,

the trees that graced the temple of Solomon.
The cedars told me of another tree.
That's why I'm here—and now, perhaps,
to learn the smelting and shaping of bronze.
The best of my tools are bronze, and hold
an edge far longer than iron will do."

Dāwīd said "You'll need a place
to stay. I have a student here
who has some room where he is lodging.
Perhaps he wants, would welcome, a friend."
He sent his daughter to summon the man,
who came at once and bowed, and said
"What does my master want of me?"
"Have you the room to host another
apprentice, sent by Shim‘on of Kyrĕnē?"
"My master knows the measurements.
I'll gladly share my lodgings with—"

He turned towards Yeshu, said
"My name is Aharon. You are Yeshu,
as I have heard beyond that curtain.
But tell me what tree you're looking to find.
And the master is right: be wary of Druids.
They guard all trees but value oaks
above the birches, pines, beeches,
elms and hazels, hawthorns and willows.
Our Roman traders tell us the Druids
sacrifice men to feed the seeds
of oaks, which is why D‘vorah, here,

is safe when she gathers nuts of the hazel,
sloes of the blackthorn, and plums of plums."

"I must admit, Aharon, that these,
except the plum, are purely new.
The tree I seek bears a bitter fruit,
Etz Hayyim"—here D'vorah
interrupted—"That's the title
of our synagogue. You must go
and worship with us on Shabbat."

Dāwīd said "She speaks my word
as well, Yeshu. In five short days,
once you are rested and refreshed
and maybe have sought this tree of yours,
join us and worship the Jewish way."

Aharon showed him the home they'd share
and where to draw water, and wash.
With the fish he'd caught he earned enough
to buy a robe with real tzitzit
replacing one the wind had worn
with all its flapping, and still had fish
to share for dinner with Aharon.

Next morning he launched in his laundered robe
before the dawn to catch more fish,
tacking across the Fala and into
the sea and back. By breakfast time
his net was full, his robe was new,
and bread was hot from stones, the fish
were steaming on stones, the jug was full.

Dāwīd had spoken with a master
worker of bronze willing to take
a new apprentice starting next day
after breakfast. Yeshu left,
walking upriver seeking an oak
which he could ask where he should go.
The one he found abounding in acorns,
venerable, he climbed into,
shinnied up its shaggy trunk,
found a perch, began with prayer,
communed and called his quest aloud.

He felt the tree move in the wind
and heard it sigh as if to say
the tree you seek for, stands in the west,
across the seas, stands in a garden
lush, well-watered, lithe and fruitful.
The boat you made will bear you there
if you are brave, if you are bold.

At dinner that night with Dāwīd, D'vorah,
and Aharon, he learned they were family
alone in Aberfala, and almost said
he was ready to sail seeking that garden,
when D'vorah asked about his voyage,
where he slept, how he kept safe.
He told them about his tribuli
and how he'd stopped using the things
after he had to heal the foot
of a thief who'd sought food for her kin.

She asked him how he'd healed the foot
"Well, with my hands I worked out the hook,
and held the torn-up bone and flesh
in place with both my hands, and prayed.
God healed the foot through prayer and faith."
She grabbed his hands and held them tight.
"Such mercy as that you showed the thief
is rare in this hard, bitter world."
She wept as she released his hands.

Next morning, his nets came up almost empty,
so distracted he was in his sailing and seeking.
He met with the master, Myghal by name.
Aharon helped with language and learning,
and working together they came to agreement,
that he for a year would learn to make bronze
and Myghal would pay him with tools he fashioned.
That night, he asked Dāwīd for D'vorah as wife,
and offered as dowry the treasures he'd hidden,
the gold in its closet he'd guarded so closely,
the mureera worth as much, or more,
and white-streaked líbanos, Lebanon stock,
well wrapped to keep the fragrances fresh.
When Dāwīd asked the origin of these,
he told the tale his father had told,
of magi come, the star they followed,
the gifts they'd brought to Beit-Lechem
and how his parents had preserved these gifts
in poverty, and prosperity,
telling him he'd have need of them,

and how he could think of no better use
and no finer purpose than offering them
for so great a treasure as D'vorah had proven.
When Dāwīd asked her, she told him she'd known
since her mother's death that she would not marry
any man of Etz Hayyim—but when *they* met
she'd hoped to find favor like Ruth in the tales,
in this young man's eyes, though their places were switched
with he as from Moab and she from Yehuda.
When Dāwīd asked her brother, Aharon said *he*
could find no objection to such an arrangement.

The rabbi spoke with Yeshu at length,
and said, though he found some elements fantastical
in Yeshu's recital yet he seemed sincere.
And so they were wed. The synagogue rejoiced,
and when Yeshu took D'vorah to bed
and lay with her he thought how this
was the way his brothers and sisters were begotten.

That year his hours of fishing, of smelting,
brought him less joy than the minutes with her,
and he feared to lose that lovely time—
but knew that the tree was anxious for him.
He'd taken D'vorah to the tree one Shabbat,
and there met some Druids who questioned him deeply,
but finally believed what the tree had told him.

He knew he would leave; he knew greater sorrow
when D'vorah bore him a squalling Yosef,

both anchors to keep him, to tie him to home,
and yet he knew they would also keep him
workways with the wind and the waves.

Fit 5

Yeshua was young when he went yondering,
sailing away from Aberfala
bound for Belerion and beyond, as belief
in a summons sustained and shattered his soul.
D'vorah, and Yosef, Dāwīd and Aharon
another family he seemed to flee,
lured by his Lord to leave, and to seek
a greater pain, its price his peace.
Coasting Kernow, several stadia
off the shingle leaving Aberfala,
tempted to turn and tack to his fishing,
return to the home he'd torn in his leaving,
yet knowing the ocean now open before him
led to the land of his future, his fate.
His ship, as it sailed, seemed bound for a shore
more wild than any he'd visited yet,
host to a lost and languishing folk.

Blown by the breath his boat sailed on,
him at the tiller turned against turning

back in this boat he built for itself
found himself following sail and bow,
flowing out into the sea.

Nights, when he slept he furled his sail
and hung an anchor off his bow,
riding the surge and swell of ocean,
rocked in billows like dunes of Tzidon
and slept and dreamt debates of turning,
returning to Aberfala, to falter,
fail in yondering, win in settling
with D'vorah, and Yosef, Dāwīd and Aharon
missing this younger Yosef fiercely
wanting D'vorah's voice and arms,
her love and her lust, his lust as an answer,
an anchor at rest riding the swells—
his sail furled when he slept at night.

This home a haven that he'd never known,
memory to treasure, treasure to remember,
riding the swells, chasing the sun
day after day off to his right,
blown by the breath of a brooding spirit,
believing he'd know when it flowed to the west,
not yet, but soon sail into the red.

To turn back now, he'd have to tack
against the wind that wafted him,
hard to tack, nothing to steer by.

Sailing, he kept his net deployed,
catching enough to keep himself

from eating only bucellatum—
or something like that Roman biscuit
D'vorah had baked from local grains,
and as he kept his heading true,
a wonder never known to him—
flying fish would flap on board
to feed him with their flesh, when the
frigate birds didn't catch them first,
a blessing he thought to thank God for.

And so he bore on sailing or sleeping,
fishing and eating frugally
D'vorah's store of sea-worthy tack
until one sunset he caught sight
of fire leaping, flaming above
the curve of the horizon ahead,
a conflagration, a great flare
unlike the setting and sleeping sun,
far more excited than settling down,
a curious flight like flying fish,
a sight he wished to see more closely,
one that disturbed his dreams of sleep,
one that faded in the flare of dawn.

And so he bore toward that sight,
eager to see this thing in the sun,
his fish hung and gutted as in Galilee,
drying in sunlight, seasoned by spray,
ignored, impatience prodding the prow
with the breath of brooding spirit

until in sunlight he saw the fire
leap aloft, lap and flow,
a river of fire fierce and flagrant,
beckoning boat and boy to stay
work ways with the wind and the waves.

Fit 6

Yeshu was young when he went yondering,
sailing from home to see the world,
burning within bearing him
out of comfort into adventure.
Before him now it flamed and flared,
becked and called careless of consequence,
unfurled, flying headlong toward
the shore and the ships shaking with sail
sent to meet this minor boat,
coming to greet and grant refuge
to one who fled the Roman fleet.

Disappointed to find no fugitive,
only a fledgling with flying fish
for trade—and news of Kyrĕnē,
of Tzidon, Aberfala, Tyros, Ouiktis—
for this they lugged his luzzu up
ashore, and set the spiral screws,
took him to meet the island's master.

The Guanarteme of Gáldar greeted his news,

seeing his shakiness shared some limes,
pressed and probed to prove his story,
accorded his little Latin respect
as evidence this Yeshu
came whence he claimed, cunningly sailed
alone in his luzzu living on fish
and bucellatum of a kind unknown.
In the dawning he took him along
to see the river of lava flowing,
not like the ash that buried Oplontis,
but red as the sunset—and sunrise behind it.
Yeshu saw the flowing rock,
delighted by its difference,
as testimony the world was weird
enough to know, to savor anew,
to celebrate its broad expanse.

With a load of limes he left Gáldar,
the Guanarteme instructing him
on how to catch and navigate
northeasterly prevailing winds.
And when their breath was held, or weak,

a current flowed in that direction
to shape the track of ship and sail.
They rode the current like a well-trained horse,
not like Bukephalous frightened of his shadow
but as if atop a tamed and gentled
mare, a sea horse mild, sweet,
bore him along until the wind

rose to push the prow again.

One day both wind and current went;
the breath told him to hold a line
tied to the bow, jump overboard
and tow the boat. He sank like stone.
The voice said walk. He tried to swim
and tow the boat with line in teeth.
The voice said walk. Seek for solid
water and stand and rise with water
beneath your foot, line in hand,
and take a second step in tow,
rise with your foot rich in water,
like walking up a sandy beach
that shelves to shore. He shed the sea
as head broke water. He held the breath
he gulped, and found footing again
in solid water and slowly rose
out of the sea, walking on water.

Between the wind, the current, the walking,
days passed, his stock of sailing fish
growing more than he could manage
to macerate as the limes diminished
and bucellatum bore him witness
that he had left a wife and home
to sail his ship at the setting sun.

He walked by islands. The people rowed
to bring him limes in trade for fish
they hoped would give the gift of walking

as he did. He gestured to show how they flew.
These fish they knew but rarely caught,
another wonder, like walking on water,
confirming belief that he was a lord
of sea and land, of sail and ship.
He could not undo these dangerous thoughts
and feared they would drown attempting his feats.
No remedy—nothing to do.

So when he came to a current flowing
strong and silty into the sea,
and heard the breath tell him to turn,
go up this broad and brownish river,
he was only too happy to jump in and tow,
washing the salt from his stiffened robe
and finding the silt nearly as solid
as sand at home. He hauled the boat,
its sail furled, far into dusk
before he asked when to anchor,
then screwed the wood into the bank,
glad to abandon his goal of staying
work ways with the wind and the waves.

Fit 7

Yeshu was young when he went yondering,
sailing away from Aberfala,
a home he'd made, a maiden now mother,
leaving them lorn, himself forlorn,
rocked by a river riddled with snags.
Awoke at dawn, arose from dreams
of holding his Yosef, and his wife
D'vorah, his soul devoured with grief,
pulled the boat back to the bank,
untied one line, unscrewed its anchor,
and started to pull the ship closer,
when someone above spoke a word.
Looking up he saw someone.

The person mimicked walking and pulling,
his posture tense—"Tell me" it said.
He kept untying his craft, but gestured
wide as the river. "What do you call it?"
After conversing but very slowly,
the person, who now appeared a man

49

in the mists of dawn offered a name:
"Misi-ziibi!" Touching his tunic
Yeshu answered "Yeshu," and jumped
into the water, walked around
his ship, the place he now called home,
hoisted the anchor, and walked the wood
into the current, then grabbed the line
and started towing athwart the current,
"Aberfala" he shouted to one,
no, many, men women and children,
hoping to get gone before
arrows or spears could injure him
or others try to walk with him.

He found a sandbar, towed his ship
onto its sinuous shifting shape,
from which he barely could see the shores,
hoisted his sail started to tack
against the wind, as the Egyptian
sailors had taught him to sail up Nile,
able to rest at tiller and sheets.
Tacking or towing he took the wind
as friend, or foe, beating between
banks upriver or towing off sand,
learning to read the riffles and snags,
pausing to rest and eat, his nets
filling with fish foreign to him,
yet gutted and roasted, restful he ate.

He fell asleep under a willow,

awoke when he sensed a snake in his shadow,
turned and found a new type of serpent,
picked it up and watched it coil
around his arm, holding aloft
its tail as if to offer it him.
He stroked the hard and horny tail
and found it loose, and felt its coils
tense on his arm, its tongue flicking out
as if to taste this stranger traveler,
and he could sense other snakes
inside of this, snakes not yet,
but feeling like him, fervent to see.

Sad to leave such company,
yet eager to follow the promptings of breath,
Yeshu raised sail, cast off, beating
the wind at its game, working to stay
in the waist of the water, away from sandbars.

By tacking and treading together, and staying
centered in the river, Yeshu hoped
to avoid attention, teasing the avid
follower on the bank who failed to bring
others to watch and pace his progress.

Moving before dawn and deep into dusk,
until he sensed a simple shift
and stopped on a sandbar to see what had changed;
slept soundly till dawn slid
across the water, and watched another
river flowing reddish-brown

below his haven and heard the dawn
whispering him to follow that water,
by sail and by step see whence it flowed.
Trusting the breath of the rising sun
he turned to the mouth of this mighty river.

Wide as it was this river ran red
and brown as it brought more soil and silt
to swirl on sand to shave from its shores.
Yeshu shook out his sail, and started
against the current but with the wind.

Sailing straight, his greatest skill
to aim away from logs that aimed
to crush his hull or smash his skull,
whipping limbs about his limbs,
a river rampaging against this rudeness.
On the third night as he slept, ropes tied,
one of the logs smashed in
his bow, and stove the carvel skin.
He leapt ashore, lifted the prow
to get it out of the grip of this log
chewing hard to harm the wood.

Weaving willows, he worked all morning
to make a mat to meet the waves
where wood and water washed each other,
a stuff to stuff against the sloshing,
and having lost the heaven's breath
started towing on sand or water,
kicking logs that came too close,

knocking away the nastiest ones,
carefully towing his bobbing craft
past snags he felt below his feet.
One day the river turned hard right
in a wide and sweeping wash of water.
Yeshu saw on the far shore
the same gesture with the same question
and towed his boat towards the person
to ask again through answering gesture
what word the river wore up here
"Wimeehsoorita" the woman answered;
he echoed back "Wimeehsoorita".

For three days more he toiled mid-river,
seeing now that some of the logs
were peopled, and came, paddled, closer
but didn't try to talk, or trade,
just floated food, or left it on islands.
Yeshu fished, but welcomed this food,
a fresher bread than the bucellatum
by now long gone. It gladdened him,
this pounded loaf of meat and berries,
rewarded his chewing, cheered his work.
Thus fed, he came to another confluence.

The breath of dawn bade him again
leave the larger for the smaller,
and once more move mid-flow upriver,
knowing himself led, but not where,
glimpsing on banks another band,

who hid themselves but stayed and saw
his splashing and splaying on sand and water.
Again he found gifts of food;
"Wasná" someone whispered from one of the banks;
"Aberfala" he yelled, hefting the offering.
And still he moved, the river sinuous,
slow and wide, but never still,
and so he moved long days together.

His wounded boat bore him at times
with the breath of the sun, with the breath of the moon;
more often he towed over sand and riffle,
past scrub, past log, staying mid-river,
till one day at dusk he tied the boat up,
dropped anchor, slept eager to wake
certain he'd reached a source of the singing.

Next morning he moored his ship, and moved
up the bluff, no path, no print leading up,
scrabbling, shinnying, scraping, shaping
his own way up, until he topped
the grass and stood before two trees,
two winged snakes, a flaming blade
that danced and circled and sang to him.

One of the serpents shied from the blade,
spooked by its shadow. Yeshu circled,
approached from its back, praying it be
calm, and crooning "Camael," a name
he heard for the first time as he spoke it,
then mounted before the front pair of wings,

at the jackal's head and held its ears,
and said "Show me a lost people,
a group who've strayed in six hundred years,"
and Camael soared and headed south
flying low and slow so his rider could breathe.

Camael flew through cloud and sun
all day, all night and next dawn set
Yeshu down at a pyramid, then soared
like a kite overhead, dancing on wind,
soaring and swooping while Yeshu spoke
to the people who ran to see the spectacle.
Through halting speech they heralded him,
told him the name of the pyramid, "Cumorah."
As if called, Camael came, and perched
on its peak, fanning the people with his wings.
Yeshu was shown the people's records
and where they wrote, inside Cumorah
and given a glowing stone from a group;
they wrote on metal that they called ziff,
on leaves they shined with sheum and neas,
two fruits they grew. They gave to him
a hefty bag for his flight home.
He told them to write no record of this
and mounted and rode Camael away.

Back at the trees the other cherub
said "Jophiel I am, a guardian:
if not for your sympathy with that snake
I would have killed you when first you came."

Yeshu stood under the sword,
caught with both hands the hilt, and stopped
the flying that spooked Camael, before
he'd cleansed his sight and carried Yeshu.
"This tree called me here from Tzidon, from home,
a call that has cost me trouble and care;
I come to cut down Etz Hayyim—
its wood is to bear a bitter fruit
for a final harvest, hard to hold!".

Yeshu swung the singing blade
cut through the trunk as if goat's cheese
were all it was, aimed it to fall
away from Camael and Jophiel also.
The blade no longer burned so brightly
but planed the shape as he traced with its point,
an upright stave, a shorter shaft.

Jophiel said "Your ship is broken,
and here is enough wood at hand
to mend its side" and flew away
over the bluff, then flew back up.
"Mount up" he said, bowing his head,
"I fear to break your ground restraints,"
and bore him down to loose the lines
and turn the screws, then picked up boat
and sailor both and lifted them
onto the bluff in his front feet
and set down boat and boy together.

The rest of that day Yeshu did

as Jophiel expected of him,
trimming planks to replace the mat
of willows woven to stop the water,
trimming and fitting below and above
and watching the wood heal the wound.
At eventide he offered both
sheum and neas from Cumorah's stash,
and each took one, to eat, polite,
but would not eat the whiskered fish
nor wasná he'd gotten from wimeehsoorita,
"A name" said Jophiel "that I have known
for many moons. Others made
a jest: the ones who ride in logs,
have dugout canoes. I hear the catcalls.
I've listened far and near in this life.
It's how I knew of you and the snake."

Yeshu slept safe and spent;
at dawn he ate, and said "This fig"
indicating the tree of knowledge
"I'd like to take it back to Yosef,
one who can heal an ailing tree.
It seems forlorn, listless, half-dead."
"How will you take it and not kill it?"
Camael asked. "I'll make a tub
from more of this wood, make it big
enough to hold the roots and soil
and give it room for roots to live."
"How will you bind this barrel together?"
Jophiel asked, and Yeshu answered

"I'll weave the bands from this mat of willow."
With all agreed, from upper limbs
he set to work, to shape the staves,
and butt, the bottom of the barrel made thick.
He shaped and bound a second barrel
to hold the water the fig would need.

Two days he sweat out to shape the staves
to fit the tubs, and fit the butts
then with great care carved out the root
of the tree, taking a third day. Jophiel
helped him hoist it into the tub
and lift tub and tree into the ship
then took the ship into his claws,
and bowed his head for Yeshu's perch.
"I know the way you'll need to go"
he said, "to sail safely home;
I'll set you there and then return."

Yeshu gave Camael a miss-you hug,
climbed once more behind the mane,
this time, of a lion, who lifted off,
flew low and slow to let him breathe,
or eat and drink, two days, two nights
and in the dawn set down on the shore
of a lake that flowed like four before it
down a river to reach the sea.
"Go build that box you bear in mind—
God only knows its use, its need,
and take the stone that shines in darkness;

I will keep the ship and tree
safe until your safe return."

Jophiel took the sword as a tongue
that seemed to shine and flare like fire.
Yeshu showed his thanks by shanking
up the shore following the shape
of a vision of a hill where he could hide
a box of stone, his tools strapped
to his back and walked, stealthily, briskly,
to the hill where he'd seen the box should be hid,
and when he'd found the site, and built
the box, he buried the stone nearby
and hurried on back, happy to see
his friend, who had kept the fig-tree watered
and kept the curious clear of the ship.

Jophiel said "I've programmed the sword
to listen to you, to point you the way.
Using your tools, make you a swivel.
Your word and the sword will point you the path."
"Programmed?" Yeshua asked the snake.
"A skill" he said, speaking slowly,
"to help us keep the lower orders,
one all who stand and attend on the gods
have mastered, as much as mastery matters
in matters of mystery and songs of spirit.
Shape the swivel to the hilt of the sword;
once it is worked, and the hilt is in wood,
the blade will blaze the path you speak."

Their parting was sad, yet a source of joy,
for each had a task, and others to see.
Yeshu was sure he was ready to sail
and keep his boat and the freight it bore
work ways with the wind and the waves.

Fit 8

Yeshu was young when he went yondering,
traveling for a tree, travailing for its wood,
searching by spirit, sustained by its breath,
learning how hardly learning was at hand,
the tree of knowledge now his task.

He sailed in the center of a slow, soft flow,
staying away from either shore
or island where smoke betrayed a settlement,
sleeping and sailing in isolation
as he had done on Misi-ziibi
and its fellow flow, Wimeesoorita.
Riding this river, a well-trained horse,
watering the tree along the way
from skanadario, the beautiful water.
The dwellers who told that designation
warned him against another wanderer,
kwiihkwahaacheew, quick to bite,
hard to fight and fierce its hold.

When skanadario started to flow

backwards with salt as Yeshu sailed,
or walked on sand or water, and met
the whales who swam upstream, though small,
yet great enough to gulp his craft,
he thought how Jonah had fled to Jaffe
to sail to Tarshish, then sank like a stone
to avoid Nineveh, seeking Leviathan,
rather than make that megalopolis
the site of his preaching, his prophesying.
Yeshu shaped his ship and his sail
for the sea again, for salt and fish,
knowing the Wasná wouldn't last.

With winter approaching, with prayers for his crossing
Yeshu knew how short was the share of his time
to cross once again the great salt water.

He spoke to the sword, said "Aberfala,"
his longing to see and hold D'vorah,
and hold their Yosef, hard and burning.
He went as before, weaving and tacking,
sailing when he could, walking when he must,
guided by the sword, spurred by desire,
the rain his drink and the fig's only drench,
and flying fish once more his food
as well as Wasná, which only heightened
his hope of landfall at Aberfala,
threading the currents and scatter of isles.

When at last he rounded Kernow's coast
he did not sleep but sailed offshore

until he reached the Aberfala,
knowing the outflow even in the dark,
and sailed to land and slept until dawn.

D'vorah and Yosef, Dāwīd and Aharon,
woke him reciting the blessing of morning,
a welcome most welcome after his working.

D'vorah welcomed him, but Yosef,
would walk away when he approached,
uncertain who he was but certain
he and D'vorah danced together
far too often for his comfort.
Aharon and Dāwīd sensed the same,
but knew why she had chosen him,
how he had taken away her hurt,
and they were pleased to see her pleasure,
how high he held her in esteem,
and heard his tales with breath abated.

Flying snakes standing attendance,
bearing the boy seeking the scattered
sons of the north now assimilated;
walking on water up two rivers;
waking with snakes bearing others inside;
building a box of stone in a berm
near the top of a hill to hide a something.
And yet, the sword that sang discord
when others approached the boat on the beach,
that burned through the night, that lured the day's fish—
unimpeachable proof that his voyage had prospered.

Word had come to Kernow that now
the Romans had reached and fortified a river,
Tamēssa, grey with muddy water,
a tidal river easy to enter,
like Skanadario that flowed with salt,
a site where Rome feared less resistance,
where Yeshu might find his scattered folk.

With little Latin and less Greek
he meant to find a Jewish merchant
to ask information about other rivers
and whether they'd lead to the land he sought,
a land in the north where Israel now lived.
His friends in Aberfala told of many rivers
but knew of none which flowed in the north
to such a land settled like that.
But they were glad that he would leave,
even the Druids who'd blessed his voyage
before, and now blessed it again:
the blade with its song, its blaze, and its motions,
unnerved them all but Yosef who danced
with it on the sand, knew it brought
his father again which gratified,
which pleased, his mother. He danced her joy
never afraid of the flaming blade.

With winter in prospect, Yeshu purposed
to sail the coast controlled by Rome
and ask at every enormous river
where it rose and who lived there,

talking with mostly Jewish merchants,
those who had followed in Rome's footsteps,
hoping to find the far-flung Israel
living and thriving, a throng of people
and not a scattered or sullen remnant,
knowing the sword would lead and keep him
workways with the wind and the waves.

Fit 9

Yeshu was young when he went yondering,
faring with a fork he fabricated,
one of three he worked for his master,
one for the master, one for his family,
one for his travels, facing away,
using the time to stay a tad longer,
lingering as summer slowly faded.

He reached the Tamesis on an incoming tide
sailed with the salt into a city
clearly, in fortification, Roman.
There he met with merchantmen,
those who'd followed the Legions north
into the heart of the Angle land,
who'd seen nor heard the folk he sought,
who knew enough of news from fellows
following that same trade
to say with confidence no such
people lived where Rome had pressed.

He asked about another river,

which one the size of Tamesis
was nearest on the mainland here.
They told of one near south across
the sea, where Rome again held sway,
so on the morning's outgoing
tide he sailed for Celtica.

He sailed up the Sēquana
to find another Roman fort
and other Jewish merchants who
knew how short this river ran,
some who'd traded at its source,
and seen a grotto where were seen
statues of a dog, a nymph, a dragon—
which made him hope that Jophiel
had been and seen the place and burned
the Gallo-Roman temple there
while ministering to lower orders,
but dea Sequana still held her court
and none but her sequestered there.

He asked what next, on up the coast,
arrived to force the tide on back,
where next to seek a streaming, frothing
flow from further in the highlands.
Rēnos, they said, already settled
about its mouth by Rome and Gaul.
He sailed next morning with the tide.

Like a bird in the fall, he feared he dare
not linger in pleasant places, but plunge

urgently on, fearful of winter,
stopping at freshets to water the fig
although they offered no further way
into the highlands. Yeshu found hope
in the words of Psalms, saying aloud
"filled with thy righteousness like a great mountain,
and with thy judgement like a great deep,"
some nights not sleeping. Sailing or walking
offshore he shed a load of shame
at having left his home again,
family behind, famine ahead.

At the Rēnos they related
word of the next, another, flow,
one with a wild name—
"wilt ahwa," wild water—
"Give me right word, O Lord" recited
as he recalled the cry of Dāwīd,
psalmist entreating and praising Yahweh,
the cry of his Yosef crowding his mind.
He sailed, eager to see this water
wild in its running, running wild
and ask again after other flows.

There were three rivers to avoid
in faring up the coast, three:
the first one small and slow to move;
the next one filled an enormous bight
rife with islands, full with ocean—
swing wide of sandbars seeking wrecks;

the third is short, and small in running.

And then a flood that flows uphill
as winter nears, as if it wished
to flee this ocean; there you'll find
mild faring for your fleet
craft, an easy cruise to lakes
that feed three rivers to three seas.
There you choose which sea to seek.
Yeshu recited back these warnings
then eased into the wild water
careful to keep his laden craft
workways with the wind and the waves.

Fit 10

Yeshu was young when he went yondering,
sailing to see the river that ran
backwards as winter began to approach,
eager to know how rumors could reach
so far without tongues to teach them to fly.

Yeshu sailed swiftly, still stopping at freshets
to water the fig and fork up a fish,
not stopping to relish the beautiful shore
until he turned into the flow of the river
and started upstream. The strength of the current
told him the river had reversed its course
days later and he at the tiller held on,
tacking to travel upstream to the source
one lake among several locked in the hills,
and here he found Camael swooping and soaring
singing of beauty, singing a welcome.

"I've followed your progress amongst lower orders.
The first thing for you is control of the sword,
so it won't affright the folk you are seeking.

Carefully take it out of the swivel
and hand it to me." When he had done so,
Camael sang in a voice full of joy,
praise in his tone, pleasure his tongues,
one head then another till all four were heard,
then handed to sword to Yeshu and said
"Tell it 'Flame on,'" then "Tell it 'Flame off.'
Now it is programmed for you to command."

Yeshu tried the sword several times more,
held in his hand, and then set in its swivel,
then hugged Camael and kissed each head
and thought he saw the cherub blush.
"What else" he asked "have you to share?"
"One of the rivers flowing out
flows to the east, to end in a sea
like that one we saw when we flew to Cumorah,
salty, with many peoples depending
on it for their food, and shelter, and flints
carried by floods into deltas, and found there."

"And is there another salt sea with its river?"
"Yes, one that flows south. It is full of rapids,
but I can transport your ship past the worst,
and very few people live upriver here."
Yeshu struck the mast, folded it down,
held to the tiller as Camael clasped
his claws to the gunnels and cautiously lifted
the boat and beat his wings the more,
careful not to rock the boat

nor tilt its prow. Yeshu took in
the view as he flew, of scattered farmsteads.

The boat was set down past the worst of the rapids.
Yeshu set his screws, said a saddened goodbye
to Camael, who wept crystal tears,
and slept for the night. By the morning he saw
that his flight had attracted the same attention
the sword always did. "Flame off" he said.
"Are you of Israel?" he asked.

The question took them by surprise,
although they seemed to understand.
From what they said, he knew they'd seen
him carried in, and seen the cherub
fly off. He knew he'd found relations
and knew that they could keep his travel
workways with the wind and the waves.

Fit 11

Yeshu was young when he went yondering,
searching for captives carried away
when Israel, kingdom of cognate peoples
was dying in hidden and desolate lands—
a search born in hope from a verse that Isaiah
omitted from Micah, who also moved south
to warn and to plead with the people of Judah.

Eúxinos Póndos the Greeks had named it,
this sea of many rushing waters,
"hospitable sea," a host of nations,
welcoming all who lived or wandered
its shores, who sought, or wandered its waters,
and thus Yeshu, from many nations,
sought news of peoples long displaced,
and found but few who felt connection
to Judah, now a Roman province,
and most of them were merchants now
like Shaul, his friend, who'd made his sail,
who lived beyond the Hellespont,

where hung the fleece of a flying ram.

A tale of a ram was told, who flew—
Chrisomallus, who carried to Colchis one Phrixus,
who sacrificed the flying ram
to Jupiter, and gave its fleece
of golden wool to a wise King
Aeeta, an emblem of his honor,
glory, and rule. He hung it in
a sacred grove, one guarded by
a dragon who would ever ward
the fleece, sly, never sleeping,
whose teeth, when sown, transformed to soldiers.

The fleece, hung from an oak, would flutter
in the breath of fire the dragon breathed.
One Jason, led by Jupiter,
brought Argonauts in a ship that Argus
built, the way Yeshu his boat,
crafted by hand with heart and craft,
a better way than something bought.

The story was old and matted, but still
it served the glory of Rome to say
its oaks were hung with golden hair.
The crew had another name, of Minyans,
an ancient tribe of ages past,
who served to strengthen the story Rome
had woven to shroud the Hellespont,
how through it streamed a hospitable sea
with an undercurrent that Rome could claim

the Black Sea's banks and bounds for her
from ages past to years to come.

So Yeshu coasted Eúxinos Póndos,
twice around the region sailed,
stopped at Colchis and heard again
the legend of the golden fleece,
how it was *here* the tale happened,
and now he knew the news, the legend
and turned from it to truths he valued,
hearing most of lesser mores,
gossip from other groups about
the coasts, and met again the merchants,
some who had known and traded with Shaul,
who told him how to hie to Tarsus
through Hellespont, and home to him.

With fork and bucket, to wet the fig,
and feed himself he sailed around,
some nights with sword aflame, and others
anchored offshore, rocked by the waves,
sleeping soundly, no Hellespont
inflaming his heart—his hope of home
of Yosef and Marta and Miryam.

At Tarsus he sought Shaul the Jew,
showed him the fig, and told the story
of finding the Garden, of guarding the fig
in the bucket he'd shaped with the turning sword
showed him the boat he'd built and sailed,
told of the mountain burning in ocean,

of walking on water, of towing the weight
of boat and fig, of finding and leaving
a wife and three children—the hardness of choice;
showed him the sword flaming on and off
and how it lit his sleep at night.
"I tamed Camael, like Alexandros;
I've seen Camael dance on Cumorah."

Shaul at last laughed at the tales
he found ridiculous, formed of lies
that Yeshu swam in, swarming like flies
around his friend, the foul brood
it seemed had settled to scuttle his dreams.
Yeshu must offer milk before meat
if he were to help his hearers to learn
the truths to free their thoughts and hearts
and bless his work and will to lead
the search—the hope to keep the hostage
workways with the wind and the waves.

Fit 12

Yeshu was young when he went yondering,
forking and fishing and filling the tub
as he coasted from Tarsus, still thinking how Shaul
could think "Flaming on" a sorcerer's trick
that *he* might employ as a hoax for the herd
of those who wander, and wait for the next
source of news, sayer of sooth.

When he could, he set his anchor close
to shore, and slept to starboard, gently rocked
by waves as the sea swung in its bounds
bringing the news of a wider world
into the Roman domicile,
one he had seen, one he had known
through tread of foot, through tug of rope,
in heat, in cold, at Etz Hayyim,
with mother and child, with father and kin,
where Rome had no hold, her roar was not heard,
and none could hurt or make afraid.

At dawn he would wake and water the fig,

fish for a breakfast, eat bucellatum
if no fish found his fork,
cast off, sail for Sidōn
with or against the wind he went
carrying cargo he couldn't release,
that couldn't release its hold on him,
the tree of life, to bear his limbs,
to hold his feet, to drink his blood
that all the world and all his kin
might be redeemed, the serpent crushed,
the anguish entered, endured, released,
the time of trust and truth returned.

He did not walk his way to Sidōn;
rather, he tried to sail or tack,
to find the wind friend or foe,
to trust the sail Shaul had shaped
and made to catch, caress the wind
hold it and shape it, keep the ship
workways with the wind and the waves.

Fit 13

Yeshu was young when he went yondering,
and sailed to Sidōn and docked the ship,
and went to find his lumber wain,
and when he found it, rent it back
for the loan of a brace of the oxen he knew,
and the aid of the lumberers loading the cart
so he could trudge to Ramatayim.

The oxen acted each as touched,
the tip of the prod, right shoulder or left,
to guide along a road that rambled
up from the beach, beside the path
he first had taken down to Sidōn.
He played that journey back in his mind,
as good as programmed there by a cherub
so clear it was, so steady of aspect,
distracting him from the hum of chatter
that edged the road and ordered his way,
the seat as a buckboard, smooth and strong,
the wagon responding to shifting weight,

carefully driven, craftily driven.

They reached Ramatayim as dusk came on,
where he and Yosef asked the aid
of passers-by to help unburden
the wain of fig and water barrel;
they dropped the fig, broke off a branch,
left a sharp stub pointing downhill
to an empty field filled with barley,
long prickly awns of the ear of grain
waving in wind, nodding near night.
They led the oxen to Yosef's gate
and freed them there to feed and sleep.

In the early dawn, Yosef and he
led the wain and oxen to a tomb
where they unloaded the wood for the cross,
the Etz Hayyim, that he would need
to bear the weight of a world's choice,
the agency that gave men choice,
that echoed Eve and Adam's voice.

Beside the wood he laid the sword,
and showed to Yosef "Flame on, flame off;"
They rolled the stone across the mouth
of stone, so he could see the flame
flicker and guard the given wood;
then led the oxen back again
and Yeshu went to find his home.

Yeshu went home to find Yuda
his brother, hoping to persuade him

to work as a carpenter of crosses
for Rome, that when his time had come,
the cross would be made carefully.

He found his mother and father there
his growing sib, his neighbors too,
all still intact, still tangled, too,
the home and the love that aligned him
workways with the wind and the waves.